LYRICAL SEX
Complete

Copyright © MInc publishing
ISBN 978-0-9865050-2-7
All rights reserved. No part of this publication may be reproduced, stored in a retrieval system, or transmitted, in any form or by any means, electronic, mechanical, photocopying, recording or otherwise, without the prior permission of the publishers.

TABLE OF CONTENTS

In the Beginning 5
Volume 1
    First Kiss 11
    Attraction 13
    First Time 16
    The Proposal 22
    Newly Weds 27
Volume 2
    Formality 31
    Good Neighbour 33
    Passer By 35
    Hands Inside 37
    Bachelorette 39
    A Moment 42
    Physically 43
    Mentally 45
    Spiritually 47
    It's all a Fantasy 49
Volume 3
    Ten Minutes Later 53
    Neighbourly 55
    In Passing 57
    Vacation 61
    Bachelor Number Three 64
    The Soldier and the Sergeant 66
    Take a Chance 69
In the End 75

In the Beginning

When relationships begin
Sex
Even without intercourse
Is the core of it
It communicates
Emotions
That will leave us elated
But the smart ones know
It should leave you sore a bit
Because for it to be lasting
You have to welcome the pain
Truthful energy
Can never be tame
Be prepared to rub her
The wrong way
And let her tell you
How to make it feel better
I'm saying
Open communication
Eventually builds
To love for each other
Sex
Talks
Speaks
But no one will listen
To the impulse I first had
To my future
I wondered about
How her curves would mould
Into our future lives
The increase in my respiration
Was instinct
I knew her

LYRICAL SEX

And our conversation
That followed was deep
My mind was stimulated
By simple things
Like how she was taking her seat
When relationships begin
Sex
Is the core of it
I'm sure of it
The way my future
Touched me
When we met
Was what I was waiting for
Based on impulses
She let me feel her
Pulse
Beneath her shirt
Fully clothed
It was my imagination
I suppose
But then she wrote out her number
Said
"Call me tomorrow.
I'm curious to see
What you have hidden
Beneath those layers."
And after she left
I continued to concentrate
On how and where she'd
Touched me
My chest
My lap
Were both constricted
Pulsing
Desiring to see her again

LYRICAL SEX

Make her my regular friend
Sounds like
The beginning of a relationship
Sex
The core of it

LYRICAL SEX

First Kiss

I was sitting from a distance
Hoping she liked me
Hoping she might be
Open to long talks
Daily
Or maybe nightly
I was sitting from a distance
Thinking she was that girl
Maybe her curls
Had been the reason
Why I couldn't take my gaze away
I was sitting from a distance
And I told myself
Today would be the day
What would she say
I've had dreams
About the way
Her arms felt around my neck
How her body and mine
Would intersect
Then common sense would interject
And say you're not her
Type
Look at who she is
And who you're
Like
From a distance beside her
I've made her smile
Laugh
Played
We have together since
The eighth grade
But that only made us

LYRICAL SEX

Friends
Not any closer
She was the vegan
And I was the smoker
She would blossom
And I would choke her
And I let out a puff
As I was thinking this over
That today
Was the day
This instance
That I'd be closing the distance
Beside her
As I looked around
There was nobody else
Like her
So from a distance
I started to walk
I could hear the drum
As I start
Coming out of my chest
I inspected my dress
And I didn't expect her
To say
Yes
When I opened my eyes
Her lips left mine
The feeling stopped time
Heart beats
Breathing
Mine started again
And I held her closer
With her arms draped
Over my shoulder
I repeated

What I had already told her
And stopped her smile
As our lips met
Explaining it
Much slower

Attraction

When I met her
She was sweat pants and a sweater
So I didn't sweat her
Easily forget her
That was
The first time
I met her
Again
By way of a friend
I tried
To get her attention
But it was her turn
To pretend
She didn't recognise
Then
We were left
Alone together
So I asked her, her name
She said
It didn't matter
Cold
No exchange
Not even banter
Then everyone was back
In the room
And we were no longer together
So I went to the back

Door
Thinking some fresh air
Would be a little bit better
And she was by my arm
Saying
"Why don't
We breathe it together."
Surprised
I asked why
She said my conversation
Was better
She smiled at my
Question
And walked out
Into the yard
To a part
Closed off and apart
I felt guilty
Because I had been drawn
To her silhouette
Her figure
Shallow
It had been the
Trigger
I told her
She knew
That first meeting
She wasn't interested
Either
"Watch."
With that single word
She let me know
In this circumstance
She was the leader
Handed me her panties

LYRICAL SEX

Knowing
I would be
Wondering
What was beneath her
Outfit
Her hands
Were taking a deep interest
Lips moist
Deeper
Breathe less
Her hands
Came back into view
When she was
Breathless
"Come closer."
I did
Taking my time
Without a moment to lose
She was now seated
On the
Edge of the table
Feet on the lawn chairs
Making sure
Her position was stable
And the new view
Showed me
What was hidden
She inspected herself
Then smirked
With a teasing bite
Of her lip
To let me know
It wasn't a mistake
That her clothes had slipped
Up

LYRICAL SEX

My hint
My tip
That I shouldn't resist
And
Her hand
Let her fingertip tease a bit
Eyes never leaving my zip
Letting me know
She really insists
That this
Could be how
We get to know each other
Better
It was an unforgettable encounter
As I would call her tomorrow
And every day after
The girl in the sweater
I could never forget her

First Time

I followed her
Through the door
And watched her
Perch precariously
On the edge of the spread
On this side of the looking glass
"I'm nervous.
It's been awhile."
I said
"And I've been
Waiting for a while.
When I first met you
You could have undressed me
With your smile."

LYRICAL SEX

She was saying this as she rose up
From the end of the bed
"So the result won't matter tonight.
You've already
Set my body alight."
She turned her back to me
As I stepped forward
And she looks back
As my hands
Reach her shoulders
Slowly massaging her arms
And she relaxes her back
Into my chest
And I could tell
That her body was warm
Lips brush the arch
In her neck
As my hand travels
To the edge of her gown
She shows her consent
Without making a sound
Her question was quiet
Barely pronounced
"What made you speak
To me that night?
Was it pity?"
As I continued to caress her thighs
Eliciting sighs
I contemplated her question
"That night in the city
I didn't see anyone as pretty.
Your conversation was witty..."
I'd worked my lips
To the side of her ear
And drew her hips closer

LYRICAL SEX

To show her my excitement
So that my desire was clear
"I want to be here.
When I saw you then –
Lips, hips, thighs –
I tried averting my eyes.
But you were already
A part of my mind.
I spent the rest of my time
Trying to find
A way to get your attention."
At that she turned
And smiled
And met my lips
Took my hands
And guided them under her slip
To her undergarments
Reminding me she was wearing
Very little
The kiss ended
As I took very little
Effort to ease the material
Down off of her waste
The cover was satin
But the Edges were lace
I was on my knees
Behind her
As her panties
Were reaching the ground
She turned around
Allowing my hands to rise
Up under her gown
Squeezing bare flesh
It was soft, firm, round
Then they lowered themselves

LYRICAL SEX

To the back of her knee
Caressing their way back
Up the inside of her thighs
And before they reached
Their prize
She pulled me back to my feet
Again letting me taste her lips
Sweet
Flavour
I applied gentle pressure
So I could savour
The passion she was sharing
As she unbuttoned my Shirt
"Since that first time we kissed
I've been imagining this."
"You were wearing a skirt
And I was impatient so my hand
Continually slipped between
Your legs."
"But it didn't go any further..."
Now she had the buttons released
Tracing her fingers
Over my stomach
Playing occasionally
With the top of my pants
My buckle
My belt
I felt restrained
As she moved her hands to my back
Nails gently pressing
As her Lips were addressing
My neck, my 'pecs'
My hands moulding and squeezing
Under her dress
Waiting my turn when

LYRICAL SEX

I could take my time
To help her lose her mind
But for now her softness
Was invading mine
"The day after
It was just me, my hands
And the lather.
I would
Rather have your hands
Touching me like this."
While speaking
She grabbed my wrist
And showed it
To the warmth under her slip
This time her tongue
Slipped between my lips
Telling me
How long she waited
For
Me
With every turn
And twist
And as I moved my wrist
I could sense her affection lift
Rise
And fall was the beat of her chest
Her hands were lowering
Her straps
Revealing her breasts
Heard her gasp as
I took a nipple between
My lips
"I remembered the first time
I had you naked
I hated

LYRICAL SEX

That you had to leave
Early."
"It was an emergency."
But her urgency this time
Had my buckle loose
Zipper down
Pants to the ground
Then I realised we were moving
Too fast
So I pushed her down
Onto the bed
Behind her
And gazed as she stretched
Her arms over her head
Fixating on
The inhale and the exhale
Of her breath
Taking action
I eased the light material
The rest of the way off
As it had already
Made its way to her waist
Her stomach was soft
Gently kissed, moving up
As my fingers trailed
And played between
Spread lips
She sighed
As a digit slipped inside
Exclaimed
As if surprised
Ever since the first day
I saw her in those jeans
Thinking of getting
In between

Tonight fate and fortune
Will intervene
From the moment
I saw my phone ring
And it was her name
I was sure
She felt the same
As her legs curved
Around my back
Drawing me closer
I marvelled how it felt
Like it was the first time
I was getting to know her

The Proposal

"What do you say
We take a trip
To the lake?"
As she paused
I proceeded to wait
For her to answer
Checking her schedule
Probably clearing a date
"How about tomorrow?
Or is it too late?"
I laughed
At the incorrigible look
On her face
"A little, yes,
But I'm willing to wait."
And our subtle
Humour
Inside jokes
Weren't apparent

LYRICAL SEX

To other folks
Since we've been together
She's been my 'Hey'
Plus like the letter
First
In every endeavour
I had made the first advance
But she was the aggressor
Career driven
I was determined
To get her
Had been a test of wills
Everyone before me
Had been petrified
Left with chills
And it took
A year and a day
To melt
Her misgivings away
Now it was Friday
On our way to the lake
She was driving
And I was feeling conniving
My hands were sliding
Up the inside of her thighs
And her suit was
Starting to rise
I was given permission
From the look in her eyes
Told me
To pull her intimate cover aside
As I teased her
The drive
Brought us closer
To our destination

LYRICAL SEX

Without pause for unpacking
Undressing
None of the trappings
Just the smooth transitions
When spontaneity happens
It so happened
Before we left the car
Her undergarments were lacking
So we barely
Made it past
The front door
Inside the cabin
She was up against the wall
Legs around my back and
Getting more excited
At the position
She was trapped in
Our bodies merged
And I could do no more
Than
Surrender to passion
Then I let her
Back down to earth
And we got settled in
At dinner I cooked
We ate
After On the rug
Before the fireplace
We were cuddling
I asked her outright
Because she was
Averse to subtle things
"Are you sure
You're not settling?"
"I admit I've met

LYRICAL SEX

Men with finer things
But I have things.
If the material you wear
Represented the inside
I can't see how a designer wins.
For no thing,
I would not sacrifice
The satisfaction your character brings."
She never left
Anything out
I had following questions
But her answer
Was what I was asking about
So I closed mine
And let it meet her mouth
Lips were soft cushioned
Embracing the closeness
We returned again
To the mood
Set earlier
Putting us both
To sleep
And the following morning
I woke up earlier
The table was set
Orange juice, tea
What was on the stove
Wasn't ready yet
Not sure if she was ready yet
As I thought that
She walked into the kitchen
Yawning
Complimenting the chef
When her plate was empty
I presented her

Her gift
Today was her birthday
I hear actions are loud
But I told her to first
Read what the words say
"To my life.
To my queen.
I've looked at my future
And it's been
Murky when
I didn't see you
By my side.
I know today is your day
But I would get
The greatest gift
If you would
Be my..."
She stopped reading
It looked as if
Her eyes were repeating
The words
My chest was beating
Sweat was beading
Needing an answer
And Before I went into arrest
She said
"Maybe."
Then got up and left
Came back
"It depends
On your answer to this."
She finished
As the box
Appeared in her hand
With a turn of her wrist

LYRICAL SEX

Newly Weds

The fantasy of illusion
Gave her a chance
To rid her mind of confusion
It had been a week
He hadn't called
That night together
They had it all
Candlelight rose petals
And the way he held her
In the small
Of her back
His lips had been
Everywhere
She couldn't keep track
But now she was sitting here
Remembering back
Hands nested
Touching the places that
His hands had been
But his had been
Rougher stronger unseen
Trying her best
To remember a dream
A moan escapes and
She checks
To make sure
She couldn't be seen
Heard
How loud she was starting
To breathe
It was a simple encounter
So it had seemed
But it had been

LYRICAL SEX

That thing
That finally slid
In between
The positions had been
Chosen to get them
Closer and closer
She peaked
Coming back down
She wondered if
It had been so long
Only a week
She couldn't do more than
Cover her feet
Her body was weak
But she managed to speak
"I missed you."
"So it would seem."
In the doorway
Was standing her dream
With flowers wine
Still wearing his ring

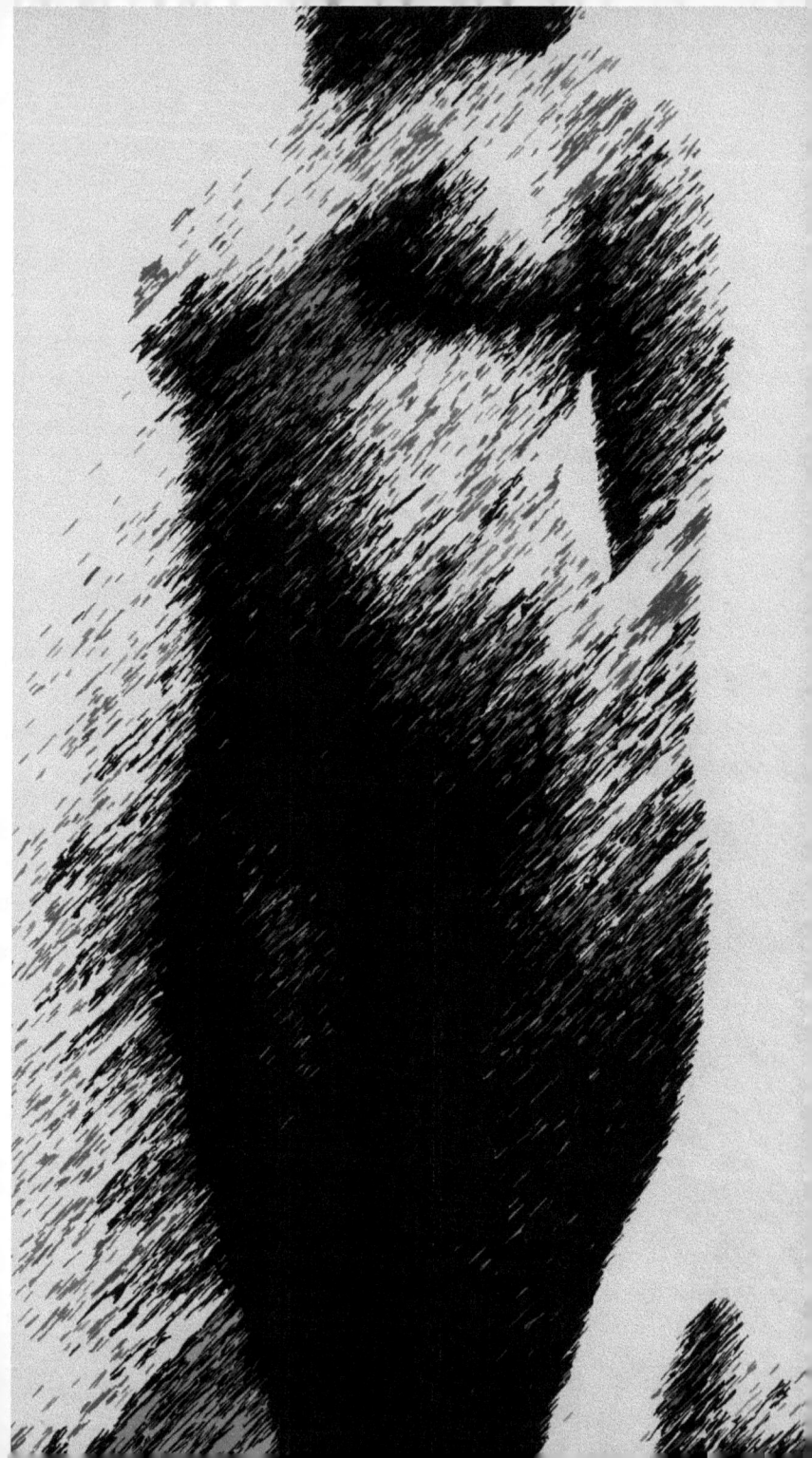

LYRICAL SEX

Formality

Across the desk
Relax
Lipstick
Business suit
"One moment,
I'll have to send this
As a fax."
She takes the papers
Turns her back
No imprint, just curves
The suit was black
Blue
Lighting
Showed a shadow
Like a stallion
Finished scanning
She's handing
Me my pages
Neatly sits
Back down
Across
Two buttons loose
See her glance
Out the side of her eye
Caught
I look around
Back to her
Composure
As she finishes my application
Licked her lips
Was that an invitation
I paused
Checked the situation

Her jacket was
All the way off
Fingers between her cleavage
Hair unbound
Excited now
As she stood up
Blouse
Starting at the top
Of her button down
Bleach white
C
Tight
Spilling out
I pinched
And it's over
"Here you go sir.
Please sign here,
Here and there.
First, please
Read it over."
Trying to bring myself
Back to
Actually
As she was demonstrating
Leaning in
Subtle perfume
Experiencing
Sudden needing
What is she seeing
Without pause
She's laughing
Whispering
"If you wait,
In ten minutes
My shift is over."

Good Neighbour

He was watching from afar
She could feel his eyes
Thinking
"Would he be surprised
If I put my hands
Between my thighs?
Would he want to
Hear my moans and sighs
Or listen to my silent cries?"
She could feel
His touch over her
A shudder
Rushed over her
Own hands
Gently enveloped her frame
Would he quietly call her name
Or was it a baritone
That would make her tremble
Feeling goose bumps
On her lower half
She had not
Yet slipped into anything
So she was sure
He could see everything
And her hands travelled lower
Impatient
He would do it slower
Start from the back
Come a little closer
To the middle
She made it
Would he say it
Was smooth

LYRICAL SEX

Would he say it
Was pretty
Soft
She could feel his eyes
Questioning
Her top
She took it off
Bare to his scrutiny
Thinking
"What would he do to me?"
Tightening her grip
Sending sweet ripples
As she
Calmed the pain soothingly
Her body reacted approving the
Delicacy of her fingers
On one hand
Were embracing the neck area
Beautifully
And the other
Was strumming
Above the sound hole
Musically
Her voice chorused
Her mind's appreciation
Of the cadence
Her body elated
The performance was
Expertly completed
But disappointed
It was at the end though
Because one day
Such an appreciative audience
Might not be
At the window

Passer By

I see her
Everyday
Walking by
It's always a short skirt
And I'm not the only guy
Whose reaction
Was curiosity
Of what it'd be like
After seeing her legs
Feeling the firmness
Surround us
Or imagined
Her shirtless
But her value was high
None of us
Were worth it
We'd probably be
Awkward and nervous
Did it on purpose
Told me one day
She had stopped in the shop
Café
Took a seat opposite me
"Hi."
Was all
I could manage to say
At first
But how else
Would you start
A conversation
She was cheerful
No reservations
Until my doubt disappeared

LYRICAL SEX

No hesitation
I asked her
Why did she appear
In the seat across from me
Which made her consider
Then wonder out loud
If I didn't realise
She wanted to talk to me
Had been the
Reason
She walked by
Seemingly, tauntingly
So we talked
There was no way
This could get better
We moved it
Somewhere
With more privacy
And in places
That were more private
We
Complimented each other
Breathing
Letting me know she was ready
Petting was heavy
Telling me
She was a day late
For laundry
Wearing no...
Drawing me along
With the way that she walked
Flowed
Over the Cobble
Stone
If only

Hands Inside

Sitting at the back of the bus
On the way from the beach
She was puzzling at what it would take
For his hands to reach
Across the seat
He was aloof
His face discrete
They'd been travelling for an hour
And he wouldn't even speak
What mysteries did he hide
Beneath
And how deep
Would he go
If they had a vibe
If they had a flow
Of words
She did observe
That the shirt was ruffled
But buttoned and tied
Slacks
Dress shoes
Jacket retired
On the arm
On his side of the seat
What would it take
For him to meet
Her halfway
"Hey."
His head turns at the sound
"Look down."
She was 'verbing' something
That was clearly a noun
With adjectives

He didn't dare to pronounce
Make noise
Caught off guard
He couldn't look away
Jeans unfastened
Zipper midway
How long had she been indecent
Or did she just start to play
This is inappropriate
He started to say
"Shhh.
You don't want them to hear."
He looked up realised
No one could see
But he
Was fighting impulses
With false modesty
When honestly
He wanted release
She judged his reaction
And smiled slyly
Gap bridged
She moved over slightly
He still refrained from speaking
But she gauged
His slow inhaling
Her hands moved
He startled
Calmed
A free hand
Helped grant him freedom
Clearly enjoying
What he was seeing
In his mind
Contemplating

How he chanced this meeting
Enchanted feeling
Then noting their
Mutual needing
Turned to mutual kneading
Eyes connected
Neither believing
She was so appealing
Her destination arrived
Disembarking
And he went back
To his seating
Both with illicit thoughts of
Next time
Tomorrow evening

Bachelorette

Images on the screen
TV remote
Changed the channel
Who would she vote for
Feelings evoked
But she needed to know more
Bachelor number one
The prince
Of somebody's son
Number two
From her friend's
Manufacturing crew
And three she had never seen
But heard
His voice
Had risen
Her anticipation

LYRICAL SEX

The first had taken her out
Late
Paid for every function
Bought every plate
Patient, polite
And was willing to wait
And the second was strong
She couldn't help
But wonder how it would feel
His weight
When matinée was over
Submerged
In the night
Way after late
For different reasons
Both made her blush
Blood rush
To areas
Unnoticed
Causing her to change
Twice
She's been out
With both
Willing to devote their time
To her satisfaction
They were either or
Perfectly typed
But the unknown
His voice
Had left her moist
Undressing herself
Feeling it brush every nerve
Was reacting to him
In ways
She didn't know were possibilities

LYRICAL SEX

And the possibility
That he could be
Using his lips instead
He's told her
In so many words
His touch
For a moment
It sounded absurd
The others were stable
Able to provide
Her with minor things
The prince had shown her
A diamond ring
But the memory was blocked out
By the tone
She held the phone
Closer
So she could hear
Him tell her how he would
Play through her hair
Then from their
Continue to travel
Through her locks
Twist and unlock
Until he reached
The mid of her back
Applying gentle pressure
Right down the middle
Strong hands moving
To the firm protrusion
She found herself
Caught in the illusion
Couldn't focus
Through the hocus pocus
Magic of

His voice
She had to know more
Before her body
Made the wrong choice

A Moment

He was for somebody
Everything
She was for somebody
In the world
17
18
Late teens
They grew older
She became a sergeant
And he became a soldier
Married ten years later
Before that
They didn't know each other
Only met briefly
Casual encounter
It was her night off
Shore leave was his reason
They never spoke
She was shy
But she caught his eye
And the uniform
Intrigued her
He couldn't leave his crew
But that didn't
Stop him from wondering
What was underneath her
Devilish blue dress
Was it thongs

LYRICAL SEX

Was it shorts
Or did she not put it on
So she didn't have to
Take it off
Their eyes met
Locked
Time froze
She saw past his tunic
Dog tags
On his chest
It was hardly soft
Every pore
Noticed
Every climate
Her frock moved
Further above her knee
Teasing
He could almost see
Confirm his interest
Then he thought
He saw her smile
Causing him to blink
And the vision ended
She flushed
He beamed
Remembering at
Their wedding
Three years later

Physically

From the pages of a magazine
Bullets
Explosion
And everything in between

LYRICAL SEX

Because she
Was my miss right
Physically
Alright
Delicate feet
And the outline
Equine
When the jeans are tight
Seams
Breaking
I think about her
Multiple nights
Questioning myself
About what else
Is like
Good ale
Smooth
Clean
Groove
I could get into
She would
Move
After a night of dance
She'd lose
All feeling in her
Extremities
Extremely
Rough
Take her through the paces
Wouldn't see her reaction
No faces
Oh faces
Come
Before
I'd let her turn around

LYRICAL SEX

Gymnastics
Flexible now
Nightly
I think about this
After
I met her
Her body
Was a letter b, d
You
Wouldn't look past her
Watching her hips
Move faster
To the baseline
Every night
She taunts me
Like she
Came out of pages
From a magazine
From what I've seen
I'd let off bullets
In her...
Keeping it clean
She seems
Like my type
Physically
I mean

Mentally

I mean
We got to talking
About everything
Scholarly
Jokingly
Openly

LYRICAL SEX

We've shared knowledge
Of how life has been
And how it will be
Will we
Be pursuing a matching doctorate, PhD
Or a business wisely
Likely
34
28
40
102
She put it together
Who
Would have seen
Her become the engineer
Erecting tents
To major buildings
I saw her more
As the
MD type
Nurse my feelings
With plans of care including
Active
Range of motion exercises
That lead to healing
So pleasing
I joked that
She'd be so revealing
She joined in
To indicate
It wasn't demeaning
Showing off her degrees of seeing
Our brilliant future
Would explode
When we come together

Spiritually

When we come together
My vision is cleared
Her perspective
I'm allowed to see
Even when
She's away from me
My heart beat sometimes
Refuses to slow
Respiration grows
Imprinted much
A lot
When our chests touched
Her breasts
Such
Velvety skin
Alone it makes me sin
So I find myself at her door
Asking her
To let me in
Nightly
Daily
She's a must
Not a maybe
When we come together
My resistance
Is burned away
And I've been known to say
Love
Not having it thrown away
Because time
Is never enough
Rough
With softness

LYRICAL SEX

Us
Is what I
Have to have
I mean
When we come together
After she's cleaned
Knowing that I would
Enter
The heat envelopes
Chokes
Me slightly
So I have to
Get out
To get a little air
And when I come back in
She's gently trailing
Her hands through my hair
As we float away
On a journey together
Elevated
Without knowing
A way down
Flying
She sees the ground
Frightened
She makes those sounds
Can't keep track her
Pulse is now
Telling me
There's going to be a reckoning
But before that
Her consciousness
Left
And we find ourselves
In another place

Sated
Physically, mentally and spiritually

It's all a Fantasy

Think about
What you'd like to see
Magazine spread
Rose petal bed
Fantasy
In real life
Takes work
Doesn't happen by accident
Rarely
Without incident
That's why we have imagination
To edit
What we don't like
But imagine real life
Was your
Fantasy
The teacher
The nurse
The preacher
Or were you afraid
Of being cursed
By your wife
Even though she was
What you'd dreamt of
Your whole life
But she wasn't down
To explore your
Fantasy
Of one time two
Women

LYRICAL SEX

You would like
To be handled in a group
All attention on you
Taboo
Thoughts
Desires
You keep hidden
And explore them
In your
Fantasy
Of falling in love
With your epitome
Of perfection
In the eye of the beholder
You would hold her
And you him
That honeymoon
Was a true thing
Whether you experience it
In real life
Or
In your place of escape
From the view of reality
It's all just
Fantasy

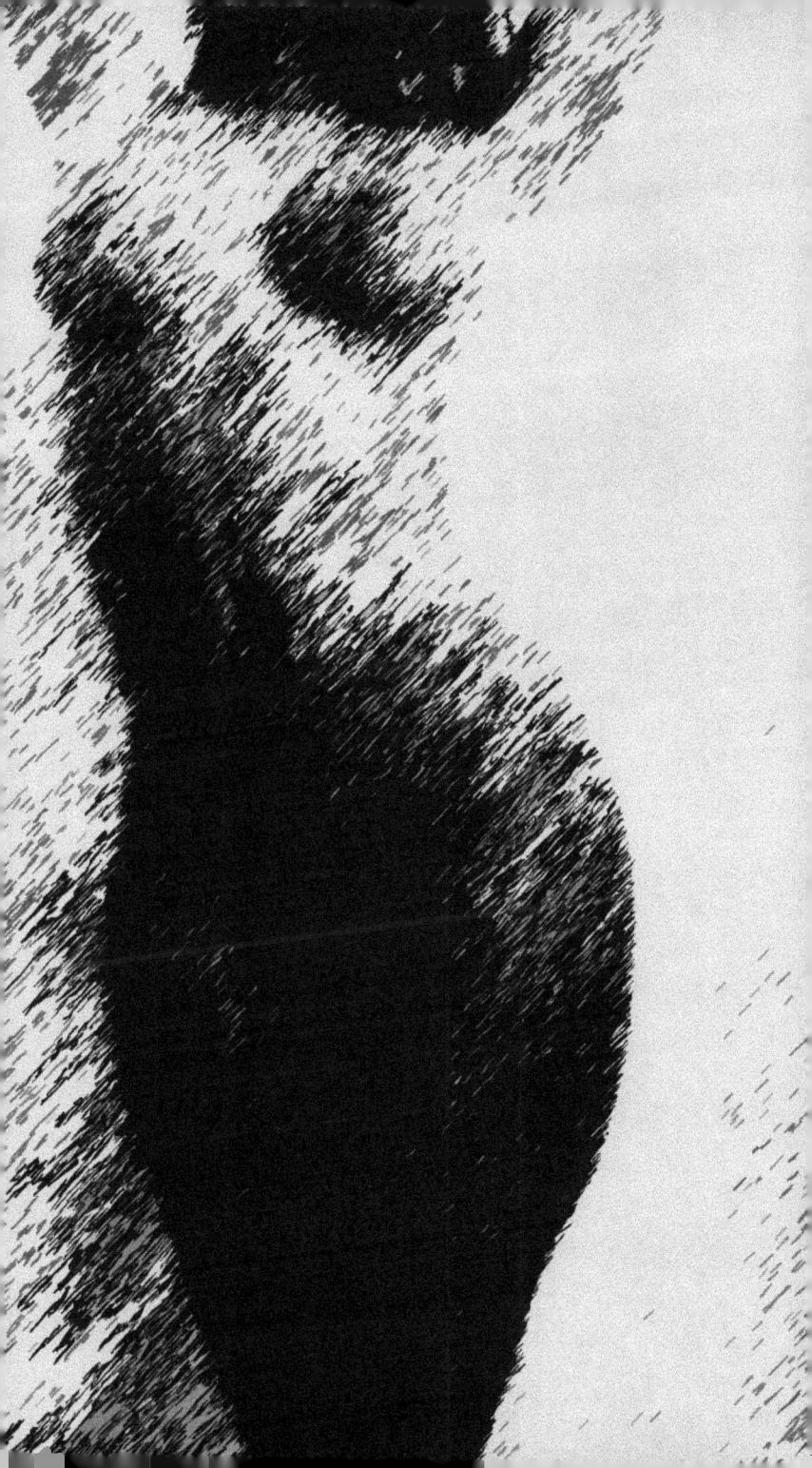

Ten Minutes Later

She walked out anticipating
Smiled when she saw him waiting
He had what it took
To be her brand new plaything
He had that look
That said he wouldn't speak
He wouldn't brag
The type
That wouldn't kiss and say things
The garage was empty
Cars aplenty
Leaning on hers like a sentry
Casually from a distance
But the closer she got
The more she could see
He was shaking
For now she liked his reaction
So she left him uncertain
Face to face
She drew her jacket aside
Like a curtain
Then it was her blouse revealing
Bountiful bosoms being bound by
A bra of purple
With flowery circles
No words traded
He tried but she hushed him
She didn't want complicated explanations
Or his verbal commands
That would only rush things
He obliged
Making her relieved that he was so trusting
By now her blouse and jacket

LYRICAL SEX

Had ended up on the top of the car
So her grip had changed positions
To under her
Suit
Helping her step out of panties
That were trimmed, comfortable, cute
She had thought in the morning
Looking at his face
She could see he was in awe and
While bent down realised his zip was taut and
That gave her a thought
Still in her heels, skirt and bra
She pulled up the material
Giving him a view
Of what he wanted to see
Saw
Her hands part lips
And nudged the nub
Causing her to convulse a bit
While pointing
Indicating he should lower his zip
Her body was ready
Foreplay was quick
Because her desire was building up
Before a finger slides
Inside
His jeans to release
Open her eyes
Wide
Was his mouth
Knowing it was time to participate
And she didn't wait
Pulled him close
Her back against the door
Wanting more

Until oblivion
Sent her back to reality
Knowing that in the morning
She would be sore
So would he
As he didn't finish
But she was already
Relaxed
Calm
Kissed him on the cheek
Patted his arm
His purpose was filled
His time was done
Before she got in her car
Made sure her jacket was on
Then she was gone

Neighbourly

"Can you do me a favour?
These bags are kind of heavy."
"Easily. Let me
Get these two
And the door for you."
Made it to the elevator
"Which floor?"
"Eight."
Recognition crossed his expression
But was suppressed
"I was heading there myself.
There's someone I need to see."
And the familiarity affected she
Coincidentally
The elevator went dark
Emergency

Light turned on
"This happens all the time.
We might be here a while."
Saying that she managed a smile
Pulled her hair behind her ears
Eyes averted
Silence so loud
His rustling was deafening
"Is your-"
"Are you-"
Both interrupted by questions
"Ladies first"
"No, you should begin."
Awkwardly it began
But after an hour they were laughing
"How long has it been?"
"Too long.
I think the ice cream turned to liquid."
"It's so hot.
Hope you don't mind
If I take off my shoes."
That she proceeded to do
Along with her tank and her
Trousers too
"You're as beautiful
Up close as I imagined you.
Since I had the view
I hope you didn't mind
That I was watching you."
A mischievous look was all she gave
She had been waiting
For him to bring it up
Having put herself under
Strict orders to behave
Hearing his confession

LYRICAL SEX

Without thinking
She hugged him tightly
Her desire
Wasn't relieved so easily
Even after their lips brushed
Leaving the potential
For escalation
His arms were as strong
As her imagination
Separated for a second he explained
"I was coming to tell you
I got a job offer two cities over
So I'm about to change my address."
His statement meant
Her audience
She was going to lose
The elevator started to move
And they were back to awkwardly
Picking up pieces
He helped her to her door
About to turn away
When he heard her say
"Why don't you come in?
Since you might not get to
See me anymore."

In Passing

It was morning at the café
Like every other
That was to say
It was already quarter past nine
But that lady
With the fine lines
Wasn't being talked about

By those who only had vision
And she didn't cross mine
I had work to do
Pen back on the paper
"I guess you didn't see the message."
My hand slipped off the page
"Sorry, didn't mean to
Startle you."
I'd have to rewrite the line
With my
Pen back on the paper
I glanced up
And saw a stranger
That was unremarkable
Belonging to a face
I was accustomed to
"Is there somewhere I've seen you before
By chance?"
"I've passed by here many mornings
And you haven't once given a glance.
I've worn everything showing my intention.
So today I was only left with
One option;
Wear pants.
What are you anyways?
Are you one of those intellects
With a weird stance
That think all women
Who wear less
Are all tramps?"
This was progressing without me
A conversation about me
And she seemed agitated
So I suggested we moved
Before our narration became too loud

LYRICAL SEX

We
Found ourselves under
An umbrella in the shadow
Of the side railing
"As you were saying..."
"I thought by now
You would have asked
Me out on a date.
I would resist. You would insist
And eventually I'd say yes
But only if
You pay for all the food I ate."
"Wait.
I'm a little slow
So I'm a little late.
But how could I
Be pursuing you with
The stir you create?
There are plenty more eligible
Besides me.
None of us here are your type.
The most we could hope for
Is to lust after you slightly.
Even if it was attention you sought
Why would I be so self absorbed
Thinking it's me it might be?"
She took her time answering
Which led to a conversation
To clear up misunderstandings
On who was being approached
And who was doing the approaching
So things
Ended up amicable
Even bought her lunch
Her dialogue was quite palatable

LYRICAL SEX

And she asked me if I'd
Be charitable
Walk her home
Since the morning was lost
There wasn't much left
In the day to lose
And after the rough patch
We had evolved into
The start of a friendship
So I couldn't refuse
Before I could make an
Excuse
She invited me to stay
I protested
Started anyway
Until I saw the look of dismay
Sitting in her living room
Waiting for her return from the kitchen
With a drink
Refreshing
And before you know it
I'd taken a day off
Refreshing
I thought
As I was about to leave
"Not even an attempt at a kiss,
Hold my hand, not even
Taking a look at these?"
Again I had read
It wrong
The words written
Long
Leading up to my departure
I can still catch the ball
So I mocked myself

With self deprecating laughter
Responding
"You're standing way too far,
For starters,
You'll have to come closer."
Before the words were finished
She had me pinned against the door
Feeling her tongue at my lips
Actively transmitting a language
That didn't include speech anymore

Vacation

It was on the aeroplane
She was at the window
I was in the aisle
Seat separated by
The time we landed
The ground was damp
Rain
And my feet were cramped
Pain
Like a gentleman
I let her cut in a line
That wasn't moving
So we engaged in small talk
She gave her alias
Then asked mine
Before you know it passed time
"Guess I'll see you around."
That was her last line
Until I was checking into my hotel
Reservation
They had lost fine
They did relocate me

Foreshadowing that last line
I ran into her in the lobby
Coming down
As I was going in
"Hello again. I didn't know
We were staying at the same place."
She was attired much different
But no doubt it was the same face
"I wasn't.
A little miscommunication but
They offered to accommodate
Me at this location."
Where she happened to be
"I'm headed to the beach.
Hoping to sneak
A quick splash in the water.
When you're all settled in
Why don't you join me for dinner after?
Room 1202."
I was about to ask her
And before it sunk in
She was through the door
I was knocking on hers
About seven
Almost by a quarter
The response was timely
Not hurried
And the invitation was cordial
To pass through the common room
To the balcony
Where there was a cool breeze
It had been a nice change of scenery
Still in the jungle
But some new trees
Before you know it time passed

LYRICAL SEX

"Let me refill that for you, please."
With that dinner was finished
As she topped up my wine glass
It was over too quickly
Longing for the night to continue
"Have you
Anything pressing
You need to attend to?"
Was the question that threw
A rope
Hope
I answered according to the inference
Trying to feign indifference
"Nope.
Do you have something
You were thinking of?"
I looked up and her strap was off
Gazing out into the sea
"I don't want you to think little of me
If my wish
Is to share with you a little of me."
Quietly
But loud enough for me to hear
Or pretend not to
I checked
The bottle
Was half way to the top
No reason to stop
So I silently gave my ascent
And her arms released the material
Fell away
As she stood up
To her ankles
And stepped out
Of the tangle

Angling in my direction
Watching her closely
As she slowly closed the distance
My reaction was instant
Instinct told me not to move
As I might spoil the mood
With nothing on
Undressed me
Putting herself above my reaction
As if it was a microphone she was testing
Then she sat down
Barely
Almost in
Back up
Down again
Repetition
Until I couldn't hear the beach
But the animal sounds were
Louder
Feeling protective my arms encircled
But she said not to hold her
Until
Her journey was complete
Sitting on my lap
With her head
Exhausted
On my shoulder

Bachelor Number Three

"Behind door number three,
Who could it be?"
Cheesy
The show
She's being teased

LYRICAL SEX

She knows
She giggles
Opens the door
And he glided in
Was that a smile
A grin
Proud
His chin
She studied his gait again
But only to check his legs
A ten
"No hug?"
Wide open
She gets enfolded and
Knowing
She had to back away
Let go
Was when her heart's rhythm
Would go
Ba dum, ba dum
"Ahem."
She snaps back
Offered him a seat
And he gently holds her hand
Bringing her down with him
Embracing the warmth
She was enveloped in
Drawn to
The spell was cast
By his eyes
Hands were placed
In the small of her back
On her thighs and
Moving up
To the sides

Giving her moments
When he took his touch away
She protested
She needs them
On her, all over
Gentler, slower
Take time to know her
Progress
Was to bare skin
To bare skin
So soft
Her body was melting
The depth of his inhaling
Sounded as if he was struggling
With the same thing
Restraint
Was lifted
His grip shifted beneath her
Raised
Then lowered her on her back
In the sofa
The phone started to ring
But she couldn't hear
Because her true desire was close
Already here

The Soldier and the Sergeant

Asking around
He found out
She was above his station
So their
One meeting
Was turning into a
One time occasion

LYRICAL SEX

Until he lost his crewmate
Best friend
Brother
It was a morbid situation
At the funeral
After
Drinks were passed
Around to dull the sensations
It was
Her brother
On her father's side
And she was on the edge
Of resignation
No longer seeing the need
To serve her nation
He sat beside her
On the deck
Allowing her to keep her meditation
Sometimes company
Is all one needs
When faced with tough calculations
Coming out of her reverie
"Sorry I didn't see you there..."
"No worries,
You seemed distracted.
This was a tough loss.
Most of us faced with
A chance at bravery
Would never have acted."
Silence between the two
As they thought about it
"Thanks.
Sounds like him.
This wouldn't be so bad
If he had taken the time

To have kids."
More time taken to think
Tray passing by
He hands her a drink
"You seem familiar.
Do I know you?"
He didn't mind
That she was slow to
Make out a face
With no name
That night in the bar
Was a long time ago
Fleeting
And if their circumstances were different
He'd probably say the same
So he gave his name
"No,
You don't know me..."
Her face brightened a little
Lit up
Maybe
Should she be forward
Or be a lady
Looking closely at his face
She remembered
Her first impression
Was improved
Today he looked so stately
"So it's not just being a good Samaritan
That made you come over to talk to me.
Are you stalking me?"
For the first time today
He heard playfulness
In her tone
So he responded in kind

LYRICAL SEX

"I was.
Do you mind?"
"Well,
This isn't the place
Or the time."
And they continued
To trade quips
Until there was a barely noticeable
Turn of her lips
On into the evening
Moving to a closed room
Turned it into a
Competition of compliments
Like how she was well groomed
And for her
It was the width of his shoulders
He responded with a bite
Of her breast
And a kiss to the rest
It was the next day
Noon
Had remedied for now
The impeding gloom
"Leaving so soon?"
He beamed down
Two years later
Remembering the seductive figure
That led to him being known as
The sergeant's groom

Take a Chance

Every day we meet people
Greet people
Great people

LYRICAL SEX

Some of them are neat people
Messy on the outside
But stable underneath people
Cheeky
Sometimes it might not be so simple
Might not be so see through
If the feelings aren't mutual
Knowing the difference
Between imagination
And a real invitation is crucial
But if rejection is what you fear
And it's the reason you stay neutral
Then you'll never move past the same
Usual
Women love brave above frugal
With an intelligence to read cues
All that might be complicated
Out of context
But if you
Encounter
Her at a dance
She's throwing you a glance
And all you're doing
Is holding your pockets
With your hands
Most likely you missed your chance
And vice versa
Inertia
Continuing the motion
Are two sides
Ladies it's often times appealing
When you ride
Tried
And didn't like it
Most likely

LYRICAL SEX

Bad experience
Doesn't mean you should
Avoid the risk of all ponies
Based on a mal experience
Should let you know who
To avoid
Because they won't let you ride
Slowly
Back away from those who
Talk a lot
But wither
When you say
Show me
Because
Without your participation
Encounters
Are lonely
Take a chance
Welcome the travelling man
Who delivers your invitations
He appears homely
But
It's those on the Fringe
Who sometimes provide the best
Encounters
Always carrying their
'Show Me'
Trying to investigate
The mystery of you
Slowly

LYRICAL SEX

In the End

We're all trying to create an ideal
Experiencing sex
How we should
Not how we think it should feel
Is a fantasy
That blurs the lines
When you know
How to make it real
The person beside you
Will need you
Feed you
Agree to
The craziest things
And on days when you're lazy
With no words to say
That's when
Your communication gets tested
You learn if sex
Is just sex and
You have nothing in common
Except for the people you've sexed and
It gets complicated
So I'll explain
Sex is a word improperly used
Materialised with a lot of negative
Connotation
We call abuse
But it's the element
The glue
That keeps what you have talking
Lasting
And if you still don't get its true purpose
Then you're too young for the role

LYRICAL SEX

Not a play you should be cast in
After you've read this tome
Maybe alone
I'll suggest you stay alone
Contradictory
Or pick up the phone
And call that person
That lets you feel grown
Free
Sex
Is an intrinsic part of sexuality
When practised
And acted
How it's supposed to be
Fulfilling
Cementing the union
Between you and she
These words
Are showers of deeper meaning
Meant to wash over you
Cleaning away the smut
So you see the irony
That this is what real life
Is supposed to be
It's not a fantasy
But it takes work
To set the stage, the plot
The scenery
In the end
It's not about the standing ovation
On opening night
It's about the longevity of the show
Solidifying that what you've created
Is ART
Immortal

LYRICAL SEX

For generations to come
Knowing what you share
Between you and your partner
Is second to none

"It is not sex that gives the pleasure, but the lover."
Marge Piercy

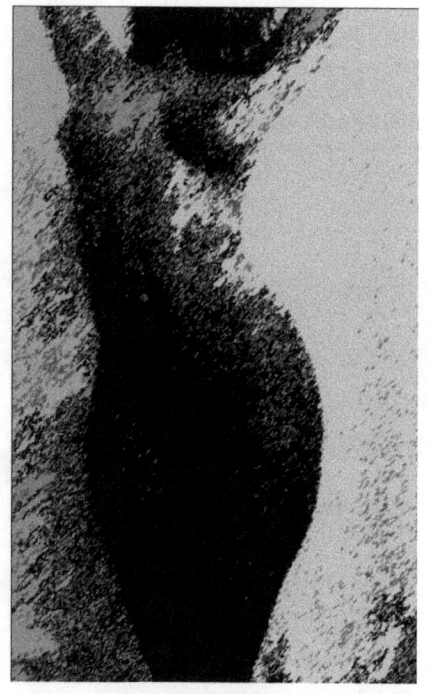

CONTACT

@infivelines - Twitter
11peacefulsilence - YouTube

www.ingramcontent.com/pod-product-compliance
Lightning Source LLC
Chambersburg PA
CBHW071408040426
42444CB00009B/2154